Maps

and Mapping

KINGFISHER

a Houghton Mifflin Company imprint
222 Berkeley Street
Boston, Massachusetts 02116
www.houghtonmifflinbooks.com

First published in 2004
2 4 6 8 10 9 7 5 3 1

1TR/0104/PROSP/RNB(RNB)/140MA

LIBRARY OF CONGRESS CATALOGING-IN-PUBLICATION DATA
has been applied for.

ISBN 0-7534-5759-8

Senior editor: Belinda Weber
Coordinating editor: Caitlin Doyle
Designer: Peter Clayman
Cover designer: Anthony Cutting
Picture manager: Cee Weston-Baker
Illustrators: Steve Weston, Samuel Weston
Cover illustrator: Phoebe Wallman
DTP coordinator: Sarah Pfitzner
DTP operator: Primrose Burton
Artwork archivists: Wendy Allison, Jenny Lord
Senior production controller: Nancy Roberts
Indexer: Chris Bernstein

Printed in China

Acknowledgments

The Publisher would like to thank the following for permission to reproduce their material. Every care has been taken
to trace copyright holders. However, if there have been unintentional omissions or failure to trace copyright holders,
we apologize and will, if informed, endeavor to make corrections in any future edition.
b = bottom, c = center, l = left, t = top, r = right

Photographs: 2–3 British Library; 4–5 British Library; 8–9 Corbis; 12 Corbis; 14–15t Zefa; 14–15b Corbis; 16 Portuguese Tourist Office;
17 Alamy; 18–19 Getty Images; 19tl Frank Lane Picture Agency; 19br Frank Lane Picture Agency; 20–21 Corbis; 26 Hereford Cathedral;
27 Getty Images; 28 Corbis; 29t Science Photo Library; 29b NASA; 30–31 Science Photo Library; 33t Heritage Image Partnership;
33b Corbis; 34–35 Science Photo Library; 34–35 Science Photo Library; 36 Corbis; 36–37 Science Photo Library; 38–39t Zefa;
38–39b Science Photo Library; 40 Art Archive; 40–41 Science Photo Library; 41 NASA

Commissioned photography on pages 42–47 by Andy Crawford.
Project maker and photo shoot coordinator: Miranda Kennedy.
Thank you to models Lewis Manu and Rebecca Roper.

KFYK Kingfisher Young Knowledge

Maps
and Mapping

Deborah Chancellor

KINGFISHER
BOSTON

Contents

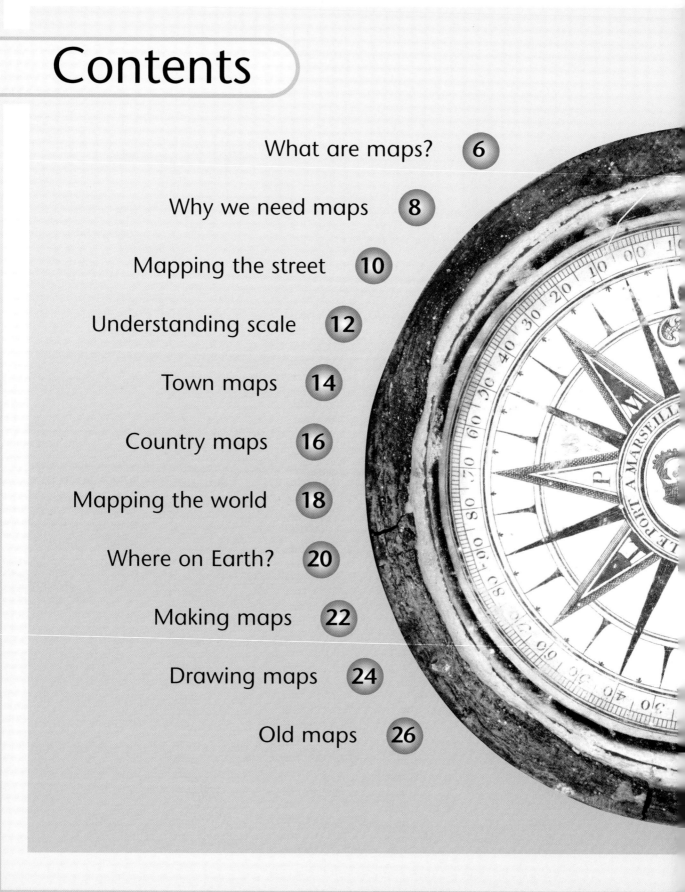

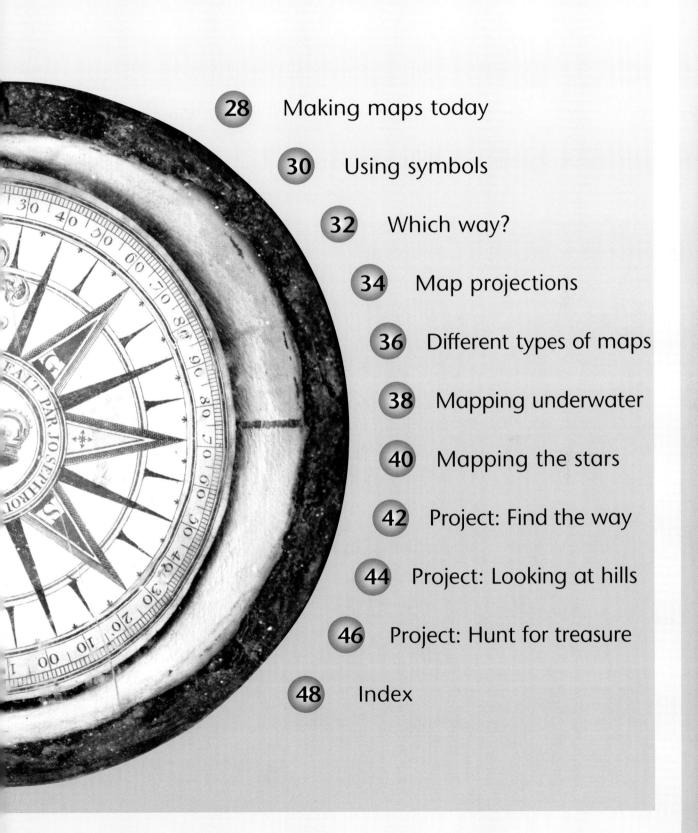

What are maps?

Maps show us what places look like from above. Some maps cover small areas. Other maps show big countries—or even the whole world.

Learning from maps

Maps give us useful information about countries. This map of Australia shows the main cities, roads, and rivers.

Finding places

Maps show us where we are. Grids are put on top of maps to help us find different places.

How far?

Scale bars on maps show how many miles there are per inch. You can then measure distances on the map.

grid—*pattern of lines that cross each other*

1
2
3
4
5
6
7

Perth

13,120 ft.
6,560 ft.
3,280 ft.
1,640 ft.
656 ft.

A
B

0
800

0
310
620

Darwin

Broome

Cairns

Townsville

Alice Springs

Brisbane

Adelaide

Sydney

Canberra

Melbourne

Hobart

■ Capital city
● City or town
〜 Main road
〜 River

C

D

E

F

G

H

I

J

1600 kilometers

930 miles

Why we need maps

Maps teach us about places. You can spot where countries and continents are on a world map. Important cities are marked with dots, and lines show you where borders are.

continents—enormous masses of land

The world at your fingertips

World maps show the huge distances between different countries. When you look at a world map, you can see how far apart some places are.

borders—*boundaries between two countries or states*

Mapping the street

We use street maps to find things in a town or a city. Street maps look down on a place from up above. They show all of the buildings, roads, and other landmarks.

landmarks—*objects that can be seen from a distance*

Flat plan

The map above is a plan of the streets in the picture. The buildings and fields are simple, flat shapes. There are no cars or people in the plan.

Understanding scale

Small-scale maps show big areas of land and water. Large-scale maps show much smaller areas in a lot more detail.

Theme park map

This map has a large scale. It gives a lot of detail.

Shrink to fit

Everything on a map has to be shrunk down to fit. Small-scale maps shrink things even more than large-scale maps so that they can show a bigger area.

Theme park

Road map

A road map has a smaller scale. This one shows where to find the theme park.

area—*part of a place or a country*

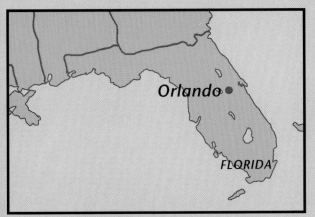

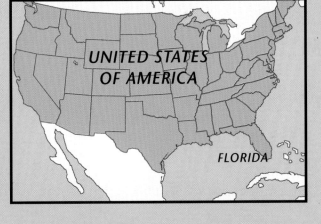

State map

This theme park is in Orlando. This city is just a dot on a Florida state map.

Country map

This map shows the U.S. It has the smallest scale on this page.

state—*a division of a country*

Town maps

We need several different types of maps in a town or a city. If we are walking or driving, street maps are very useful. Bus or train maps help us plan our journeys on public transportation.

Finding the way

Tourist maps are sometimes in 3-D. They illustrate the landmarks in a city. The red line on this map shows the route a tourist has planned to find his or her way around.

Street map

Buildings and roads look very small on maps, but they are much bigger in real life. This busy street in Paris would look very different on a street map.

Train map

On maps of the Metro (subway) in Paris, France, train routes are shown with lines. Each route has its own color and number. The names of all of the stations are marked on the map.

Country maps

Maps of countries cover large areas. They show important features such as mountains, cities, and borders. Symbols on country maps show points of interest.

Capital city

The red dots on this map are capital cities. Lisbon is the capital of Portugal. It was built around a natural harbor.

PORTUGAL

Lisbon

capital city—most important city in a country

Natural border

These mountains form a natural border between Spain and France. They are in a mountain range called the Pyrenees.

FRANCE

Pyrenees

Borders between countries are marked with a red line

SPAIN

● **Madrid**

	Flamenco dancing
	Fishing
	Wine making
	Orange growing
	Water sports
	Tourist area

Mapping the world

World maps are covered with a grid of lines. These are lines of latitude and longitude. We use them to figure out the exact position of places.

Starting at Greenwich

The "Greenwich meridian" is the line of longitude that passes through Greenwich, England. It marks 0° (degrees) longitude. All other lines of longitude are measured either east or west of this line.

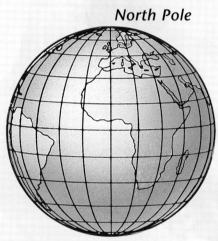

North Pole

South Pole

latitude—distance north or south of the equator

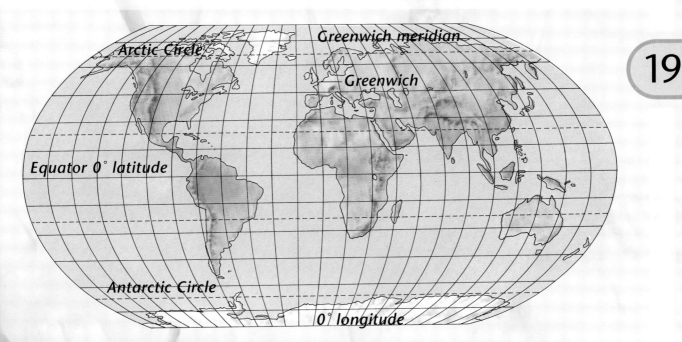

Arctic Circle

Greenwich meridian

Greenwich

Equator 0° latitude

Antarctic Circle

0° longitude

At the poles

All lines of longitude meet at the North and South poles. These penguins live in the Antarctic—the frozen continent around the South Pole in the Antarctic Circle.

In the middle

The equator is an imaginary line that runs around the middle of Earth. All lines of latitude are measured either north or south of the equator.

longitude—*distance east or west of the Greenwich meridian*

Where on Earth?

Any position on Earth can be described using measurements of latitude and longitude. Grids on maps help us find a particular place such as a city on a world map or buried gold on a treasure map.

Global address

A city's position of latitude and longitude is like an "address" on a world map. New Orleans in Louisiana is 30° north and 90° west.

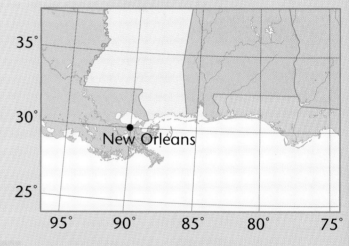

New Orleans

Paddling out to sea

The famous Mississippi river flows through New Orleans and out into the sea. This busy route for river traffic is more than 3,720 miles long.

position—*exact place where something is*

Finding hiding places

Even treasure maps have
grids marked on them.
Any place or thing on
the map can be given
a "grid reference"
using letters and
numbers at the
edge of the grid.

A   B
C
D

8

7

6

5

4

3

Forest
River
Beach
Mountain
Volcano
Lake
Swamp
Treasure

N
W   E
S

B

C

Making maps

Five hundred years ago a lot of the world was unexplored. Brave people discovered unknown lands and made the first maps of the places that they found.

Voyages of discovery

Explorers learned as much as they could about coastlines. They used special equipment to find their way and to make maps.

Finding the right way

Compasses helped explorers sail in the right direction. Maps were drawn with north at the top and south at the bottom.

compass

quill pen

Are we there yet?

The distance a ship had to travel was measured on a map using a pair of dividers.

Where are we now?

Sailors used a sextant to figure out how far north or south of the equator they were.

sextant

dividers

Drawing maps

You need a lot of information about the landscape to draw an exact and correct map. Many measurements need to be taken such as the heights of mountains and the lengths of rivers.

Surveying the land

Surveyors are people who measure features of the landscape so that maps can be made. They record every detail, for example whether it is woody or bare, dry or marshy.

Contour lines

On some maps hills and mountains are shown with "contour lines." These lines connect all of the land that is the same height. The closer the lines, the steeper the slope.

landscape—*area of the countryside*

Old maps

People have been making maps for thousands of years. The first maps of the whole world were made around 1,800 years ago. They only show countries and oceans that people knew about at the time.

What's missing?

The first mapmakers did not know that the Americas, Australia, and the Antarctic existed. This map shows what some people thought the world looked like around 900 years ago.

Changing maps

World maps changed when new countries were found. This map was made around 100 years after North America was first "discovered."

Modern map

This is a modern map of the world. There are no new lands left to explore, and we know what all of the continents look like. Today nothing is missing from our maps.

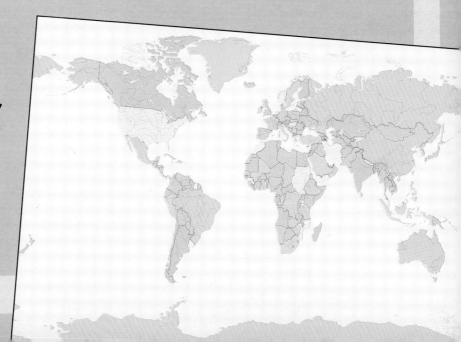

ocean—a large sea

Making maps today

New technology helps us make maps. Photographs of land and water can be taken from aircraft and satellites. Cartographers use these images along with other information to create maps.

Using computers

Today cartographers use computers to help them make maps. A lot of geographical data can be stored on a database and used to create many different types of maps. This is a digital map of part of Asia.

Eyes in the sky

This is a Russian space satellite, circling high above Earth. Data from many satellites is sent back to Earth and is used to make maps.

Looking down

The Amazon river in northern Brazil looks like this from space. The dark areas are rain forests, and the river is a thin, yellow line. Satellite photographs give cartographers a detailed picture of the landscape.

cartographers—*people who draw maps*

Using symbols

Maps need to crowd a lot of information into a small space. Symbols and colors on maps are used to show many different things on the ground.

Flying over London, England

This is bird's-eye view of London's downtown. Street maps of the area show all of the roads, buildings, and parks. Symbols tell us what important buildings are used for.

Map key

Symbols and colors used on maps are explained in the key. We need to look at the key to understand what the map is showing us.

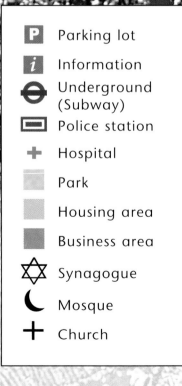

P	Parking lot
i	Information
⊖	Underground (Subway)
▭	Police station
+	Hospital
▮	Park
▮	Housing area
▮	Business area
✡	Synagogue
☾	Mosque
✝	Church

***bird's-eye view**—picture of something from above*

Up close

This map shows
a small area of the
satellite photo. Different
colors show how land
is used, for example
for houses or parks.

key—explanation of symbols on a map

Which way?

Whichever way you look you are facing in a particular direction. This will be somewhere between north, south, east, and west. You use a compass to find your direction.

Map reading

These hikers are using a compass with a map. They turn the map around so that the north arrow lines up with the compass needle.

Pointing the way

All maps have an arrow or a "compass rose" on them showing north. In Lisbon, Portugal, as well as in other places, the compass directions are shown on the ground, too.

Go north

You need to use a compass to discover which way is north. A compass has a magnetic needle that always points toward the north.

Map projections

The most accurate world maps are globes because they show the land and water as it really is. Flat maps change the shape of some countries.

Projections

The way that we show curved Earth on a flat map is called a projection. The projection on the right is the "Mercator" projection.

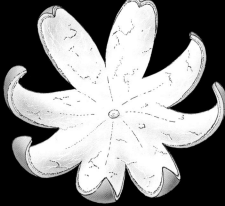

Flat map

A globe can be split apart into segments and "peeled" like an orange. The segments are placed side by side to make a flat map that looks like this.

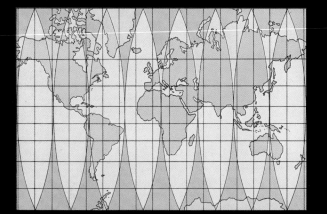

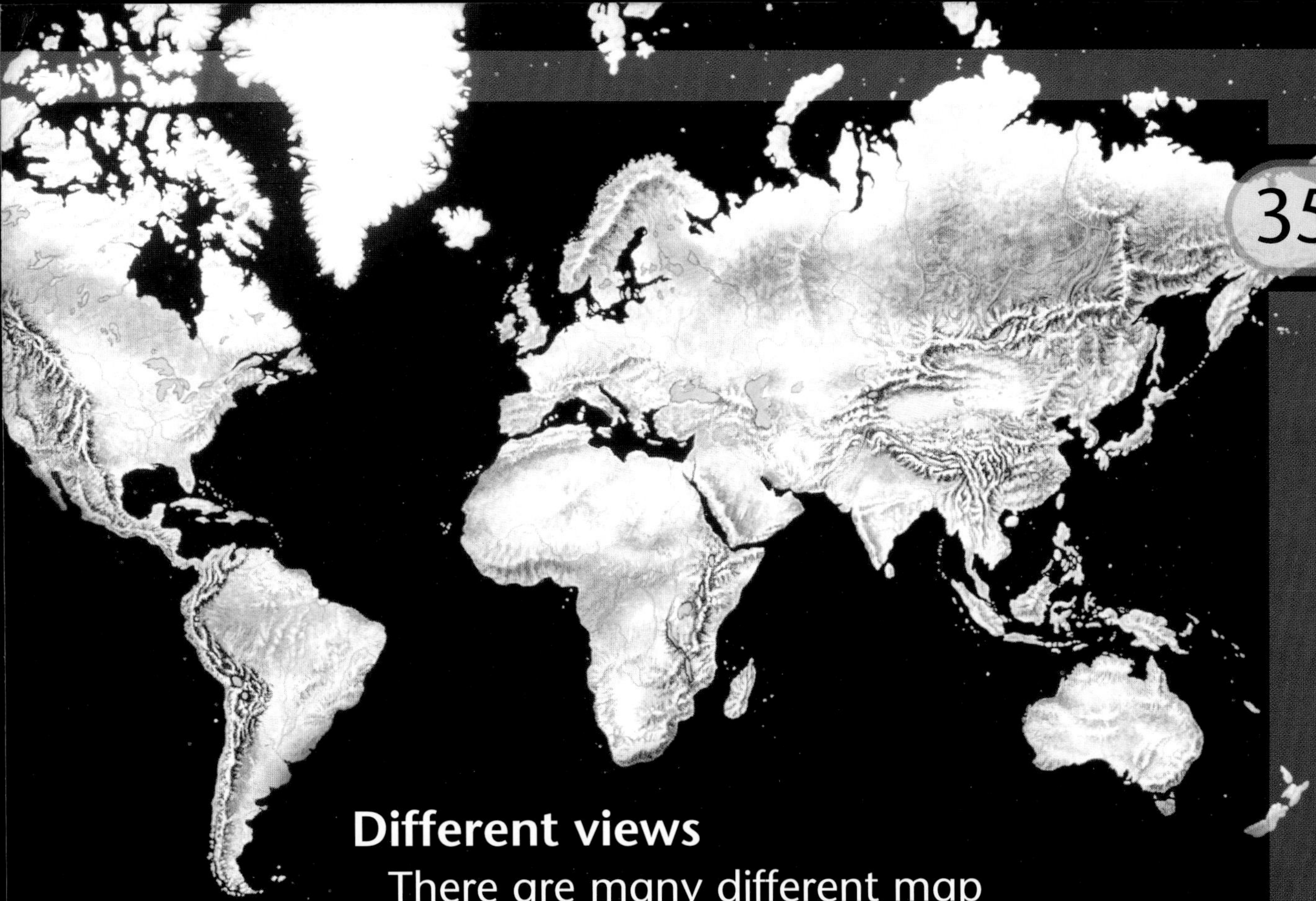

Different views

There are many different map projections. The one shown below splits the globe up in a special way so that countries and oceans are not too distorted.

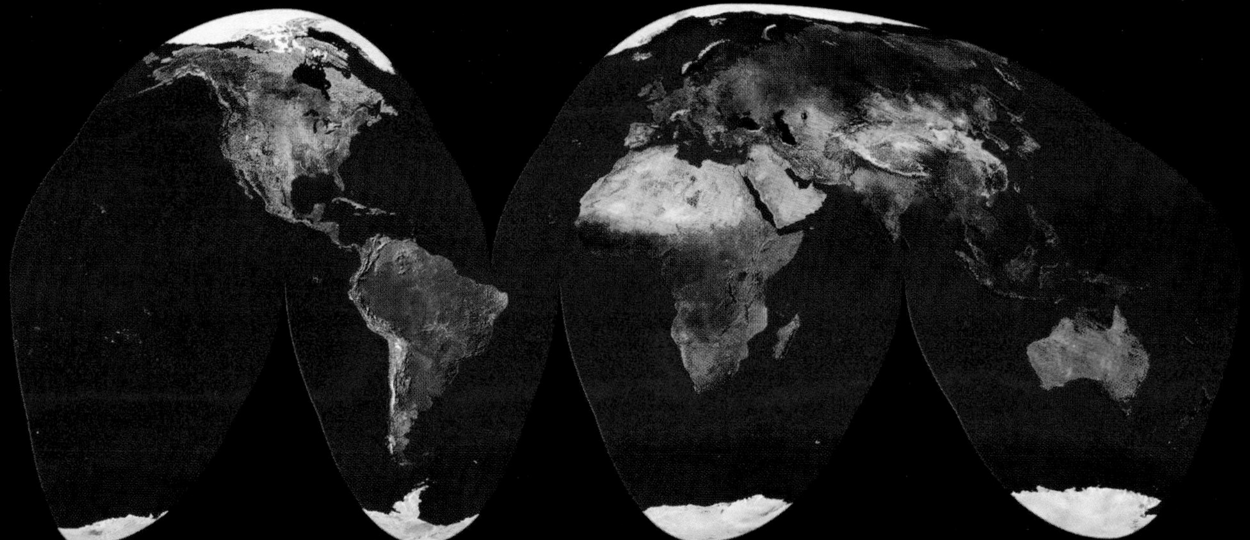

distorted—changed from usual shape

Different types of maps

There are many types of maps. Maps can give information about things such as the weather. They can also show how places compare with each other.

Underwater maps

Maps of the sea are called charts. They help boats follow routes and avoid danger. The crosses on this chart stand for shipwrecks on the seabed.

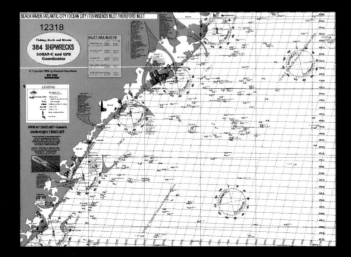

chart—*map of the sea, sky, or space*

Mapping the weather

Weather maps tell
us what the weather
is like in a particular place.
Symbols are used to show
different types of weather.
The symbols here show sun,
clouds, rain, and tornadoes.

Night-lights

This world map
was made using
several satellite photos.
It shows which parts of
the world use the most
electric light at night.

routes—*ways to go to get to a place*

Mapping underwater

There are huge mountains and deep canyons under the sea. Measurements of these features are taken so that maps showing the ocean floor can be made.

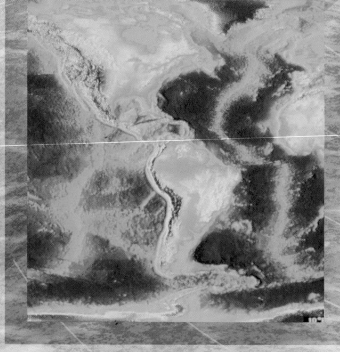

Ocean ridges
Underwater mountain ranges are called ocean ridges. They can be very long. On this map the deepest water is dark blue. The ocean ridges are the lightest blue.

ridges—*ranges of mountains*

Deep blue sea

Special equipment measures how long sound takes to reach the seabed and bounce back again. The depth of the water can then be figured out.

Diving for data

Deep-sea submersibles are small submarines that take divers down to explore the seabed. Measurements are taken by divers to provide data for maps.

submersibles—*craft that can travel underwater*

Mapping the stars

People who study stars in the sky are called astronomers. Today's astronomers look at distant galaxies through powerful telescopes. Then they make space maps called star charts.

Seeing stars

You can look at the stars with a regular pair of binoculars. Some constellations can be seen from the northern half of the world, and others can be seen from the south.

galaxies—*very large groups of stars*

Star charts

A long time ago people named constellations after animals, heroes, and gods. They painted beautiful charts to show the position of the stars in the sky.

Mapping the Moon

Maps are made of the Moon, as well as of Earth. Photographs are used to make maps of the craters, valleys, and canyons on the surface of the Moon.

constellations—groups of stars

Find the way

Make your own compass

A compass needle is a magnet that points north. You can turn a needle into a magnet and float it in water to make a compass.

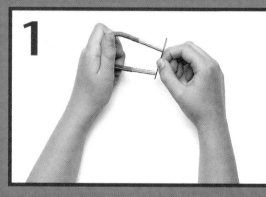

1

Hold the needle and gently rub it with the magnet. Do this around 50 times, always rubbing in the same direction.

You will need
- Large needle
- Magnet
- Cork
- Tub of water
- Compass

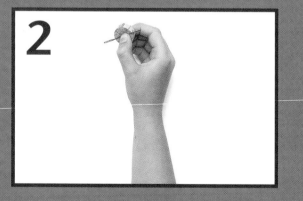

2

Ask an adult to cut a slice of cork for you. Carefully balance your needle on top of the cork and float it in a tub of water.

3

Place a compass next to your floating needle. Both "compass needles" should be facing the same direction—north!

Mapping your bedroom

You can draw a map of your bedroom using your footsteps to measure what is there. Count how many footsteps it takes for you to walk the length and width of your room. You will need some paper, a ruler, and some markers or pens to make your map.

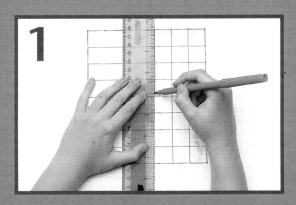

Draw an outline of your room. Fill it in with a grid. Each square on the grid stands for one footstep.

Measure your furniture in footsteps. Draw furniture shapes on your map, putting them in the right places.

3

window

door

Add the door and window. Color in all the furniture using markers or pens. You can draw a map key to explain your colors.

Looking at hills

Make a relief map

Some maps use color shading and modeling to show how land varies in height. Mountains and valleys are easy to see on a relief map. You can make a relief map using craft materials.

Roll up three balls of newspaper. Make each ball a different size. Stick the balls firmly to the thick cardboard using tape.

You will need
- Newspaper
- Sheet of thick cardboard
- Tape
- Scissors
- Glue or wallpaper paste
- Paper towel
- Poster paints
- Paintbrush

Cut some pieces of newspaper into thin strips. Glue the strips over the top of the newspaper balls. Add several layers and then leave them to dry.

3

4

Glue a layer of paper towels over the map. Remember to cover the cardboard base as well as the "hills." Leave it to dry.

Paint your map with bands of color. Use a new color to show different heights. Land of the same height should be the same color.

On this map green shows low ground. Yellow shades stand for medium height, while dark brown means higher ground.

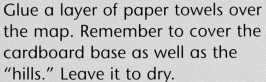

Hunt for treasure

Make a treasure map

In stories old maps of desert islands help people find buried treasure. Make your own treasure map for a make-believe island.

Scrunch up a piece of paper into a loose ball. Flatten it out again with your hands.

You will need
- Paper
- Poster paints
- Paintbrush
- Pencil
- Ruler
- Markers or pens
- Scissors

Dilute some green or brown paint to make it very watery. Paint this over the whole sheet of crumpled paper. Leave it to dry.

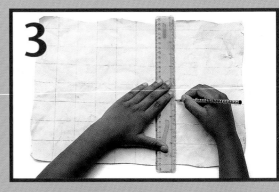

Draw a grid of squares across the paper with a pencil and a ruler. Each line should be the same distance apart.

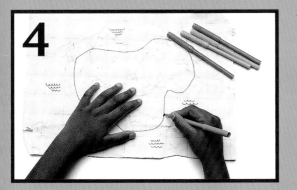

4

Draw the outline of a desert island. Make it an interesting, unusual shape. Add some waves to show where the sea is.

5

Draw some pictures on your map to stand for different things such as lakes and volcanoes. Make the symbols small and simple.

6

Draw a key to explain your symbols and add a north arrow. Shade in the edges to make the map look old.

Ask your friends to figure out where the treasure is buried.

Index